CHRISTIAN HEROES: THEN & NOW

ADONIRAM JUDSON

I0889104

Unit Study

Curriculum Guide

JANET & GEOFF BENGE

YWAM PUBLISHING
P.O. BOX 55787 SEATTLE, WA 98155

YWAM Publishing is the publishing ministry of Youth With A Mission. Youth With A Mission (YWAM) is an international missionary organization of Christians from many denominations dedicated to presenting Jesus Christ to this generation. To this end, YWAM has focused its efforts in three main areas: (1) training and equipping believers for their part in fulfilling the Great Commission (Matthew 28:19), (2) personal evangelism, and (3) mercy ministry (medical and relief work).

For a free catalog of books and materials, contact:

YWAM Publishing
P.O. Box 55787, Seattle, WA 98155
(425) 771-1153 or (800) 922-2143
www.ywampublishing.com

Adoniram Judson: A Unit Study Curriculum Guide

10 09 08 07 06 05 04 10 9 8 7 6 5 4 3 2 1

Published by Youth With A Mission Publishing
P.O. Box 55787
Seattle, WA 98155

ISBN 1-57658-276-0

Verses marked KJV are taken from the King James Version of the Bible.

Verses marked NIV are taken from the Holy Bible, New International Version®, Copyright © 1973, 1978, 1984 by the International Bible Society. Used by permission of Zondervan Publishing House.

Printed in Germany.

Contents

Adoniram Judson

1788–1850

Adoniram Judson: A Unit Study Curriculum Guide

This unit study guide is designed to accompany the book *Adoniram Judson: Bound for Burma* from the Christian Heroes: Then & Now series by Janet and Geoff Benge. It provides the Christian schoolteacher and homeschooling parent with ways to use the book as a vehicle for teaching or reinforcing various curriculum areas, including

- Creative writing.
- Drama.
- Movie critiquing.
- Reading comprehension.
- Essay writing.
- History and geography concepts.

As there are more ideas than could possibly be used in one unit, it is the parent/teacher's job to sift through the ideas and select those that best fit the needs of the student or students.

The activities recommended in this unit study guide are

- Reflective of a wide range of learning styles.
- Designed for both group and individual study.
- Suitable for a range of grade levels and abilities.

Learning Styles

Choose those activities that are best suited to your student or students. For example, when studying the physical features of a country, a kinesthetic learner will learn best by producing a three-dimensional clay model representing the physical features of the country, whereas a visual learner will find it more meaningful to produce a poster map of the country for the classroom wall.

Group or Individual Study

While the activities contained in this unit study guide are designed to be carried out by a student working alone, instructions are also provided for adapting an activity for a group.

Grade Levels/Abilities

As you thumb through this unit study guide, you will note that grade levels are not assigned to particular activities, though some areas—essay topics, for example—progress from the simple to the complex. This approach has been taken because students of varying grade levels can undertake most of the activities. For example, one of the activities suggests: “Create a television documentary called *Myanmar, the Unknown Land*. Start by interviewing a selection of people to find out what they know (or don’t know) about Burma (now commonly known as Myanmar). Then use videotape, posters, photographs, and commentary to teach viewers about the country." A fourth grader completing this activity would tend to focus on concrete questions, such as "Do you know where Burma is?" and "Do you know what the Burmese call their country today?" A tenth grader would be able to process more abstract questions, such as "On a world scale, where do you think Myanmar would be placed by the UN for human rights violations?" and "What form of government do you think Myanmar has?" Each student uses the same activities and instructions to create work appropriate to his or her age and cognitive ability.

In the center of this unit study guide you will find two foldout pages. These pages contain three maps and a fact sheet to be filled out by the student. The maps and fact sheet are designed to be photocopied onto individual pages so that each student can store them in his or her folder. They are for use with the social studies section of this unit study guide (chapter 6).

Before you begin teaching from this unit study guide, please read through each section. You may wish to highlight the activities that appeal to you or that your students would enjoy or be challenged by. Many teachers find it useful to plan the culminating event (see chapter 8) first and then select a range of learning activities that lend themselves to this event.

For the sake of brevity in the instructions that accompany each section, the word *teacher* includes the homeschooling parent, and the word *student* refers to a child either in a traditional classroom or in a homeschool environment.

— 1 —

Key Bible Verses

The authors have selected four Bible verses that can be used alongside or as part of this unit study. For your convenience, these verses have been quoted in two versions: the King James Version and the New International Version. Of course, many other appropriate Bible verses can be added to the list if more are needed. The verses could be used in the following ways:

Memorization. The teacher can assign one or all of the verses to be memorized during the course of the study. A chart could track which students have memorized which verses.

Meaning. The verses can be used to spark conversation on spiritual aspects of Adoniram Judson's life. This can then be translated into action by having students form groups and present one of the verses to the class in a creative manner. Students could make up a skit to illustrate the meaning of the verse or present a one-act play to illustrate how the verse was relevant in the life of Adoniram Judson.

Devotional. The teacher might consider beginning a class or family devotional book. To do this, the teacher should familiarize the students with a variety of devotional writings and then ask them to write a devotion based upon their own understanding of one of the verses as it relates to the life of Adoniram Judson. The pages could then be glued or copied into a blank book, illustrated, and signed. The various devotions could be read aloud at appropriate times, including during assemblies and family devotional times and at the culminating event.

Display. Students could design a plaque, wall hanging, or banner, with one of the verses written on it. This could be hung in a prominent place while the unit study is underway and used for decoration during the culminating event.

"Yea, though I walk through the valley of the shadow of death, I will fear no evil: for thou art with me; thy rod and thy staff they comfort me" (Psalm 23:4 KJV).

"Even though I walk through the valley of the shadow of death, I will fear no evil, for you are with me; your rod and your staff, they comfort me" (Psalm 23:4 NIV).

"Trust in the LORD with all thine heart; and lean not unto thine own understanding. In all thy ways acknowledge him, and he shall direct thy paths" (Proverbs 3:5–6 KJV).

“Trust in the LORD with all your heart and lean not on your own understanding; in all your ways acknowledge him, and he will make your paths straight” (Proverbs 3:5–6 NIV).

“Therefore I say unto you, take no thought for your life, what ye shall eat, or what ye shall drink; nor yet for your body, what ye shall put on. Is not the life more than meat, and the body than raiment?” (Matthew 6:25 KJV)

“Therefore I tell you, do not worry about your life, what you will eat or drink; or about your body, what you will wear. Is not life more important than food, and the body more important than clothes?” (Matthew 6:25 NIV)

“Whom resist stedfast in the faith, knowing that the same afflictions are accomplished in your brethren that are in the world” (1 Peter 5:9 KJV).

“Resist him, standing firm in the faith, because you know that your brothers throughout the world are undergoing the same kind of sufferings” (1 Peter 5:9 NIV).

2

Display Corner

Many students will enjoy collecting and displaying objects related to the country or culture they are studying. It is motivational to designate a corner of the room, including a table or desk and wall space, that can be used for this purpose. Keep some index cards on the table and encourage students to label their contributions, including as much information as possible about where each object came from, what it is used for, and who would use it.

Encourage students to ask their parents and friends if they have anything relevant (but not valuable) from Myanmar that they could bring to class. A visit to an Asian grocery could also yield some very interesting display items, as would a trip to the local library to find books on Myanmar and famous Burmese people and events. (See the Books and Resources section for ideas.) Following is a list of items students (or you) might like to display. Of course, there are many more options.

- A large map of Myanmar
- A Burmese flag
- Picture books on Myanmar
- Burmese food that students might not be familiar with, such as eggplant, okra, chayote, avocados, mangoes, jackfruit, and a variety of spices (available at an Asian grocery store)
- Articles about the treatment of Christians (and about human rights in general) in Myanmar today
- Examples of Burmese writing, including Bibles and tracts (The Judson Bible, which Adoniram Judson translated, is available through International Bibles via telephone 402-453-2401 or at http://internationalbibles.com/catalog/bibles/publishers/abs/103789.htm. A printable online Bible tract is available at www.chick.com; search for "Burmese.")
- Photographs and articles about Myanmar, both in the past and in the present (Many of these can be downloaded from the websites listed in the Books and Resources section or at http://search.asiaco.com/Myanmar/Personal_Home_Pages/.)
- Dolls in native Burmese dress
- Articles or books about ships in the eighteenth and nineteenth centuries

3

Chapter Questions

There are four questions related to each chapter of *Adoniram Judson: Bound for Burma:*

1. A vocabulary question drawn from the text and referenced to a page in the book
2. A factual question arising from the text
3. A question to gauge the level of a student's comprehension
4. An open-ended question seeking an opinion or interpretation

These questions are designed for students to complete on their own. They are best answered after a student finishes reading each chapter in the book. Answers to the first three questions for each chapter are given in Appendix B of this guide. The answer to the fourth question is open-ended and needs to be evaluated separately. Since question four deals with a student's interpretation or opinions, it is a good question on which to base a group discussion. Keep in mind that there are no right or wrong answers to question four, only positions a student should be able to justify.

To gain maximum benefit from the questions, the students should write full-sentence answers and not just one or two words. For example, in response to the question "What did Adoniram's father do for a living?" students should write, "Adoniram's father was a preacher," and not just "preacher."

Each vocabulary question asks the students to use the new word in a sentence. Make sure their sentences clearly demonstrate the meaning of the vocabulary word.

As a supplement to answering the questions, students may write a short summary of each chapter or write a response to the chapter in their journal. This could involve the students writing about how they relate to Adoniram Judson's actions, noting how they think they would react in a similar situation, and speculating as to what might happen next in the story.

Chapter One

1. What are gunwales (page 13)? Use this word in a sentence.
2. What language did the other two passengers on the *Packet* speak?
3. Why was it especially dangerous to be aboard a British ship?
4. Why do you think the American Board thought it needed the London Missionary Society's help?

Chapter Two

1. What is an enigma (page 17)? Use this word in a sentence.

2. What did Adoniram's father do for a living?
3. Why did Adoniram freeze in terror when he saw the letter in his father's hand?
4. Adoniram wondered what a "great" man was (page 21). In your opinion, what makes a person great?

Chapter Three

1. What does *iniquity* mean (page 30)? Use this word in a sentence.
2. How did Adoniram get from Albany to New York City?
3. Why would Adoniram's admission to his father that he was a Deist have put an end to his college career?
4. Do you think it was inevitable that Adoniram would have one day clashed with his father? Why or why not?

Chapter Four

1. What is a chaplain (page 45)? Use this word in a sentence.
2. On what date did Adoniram become a Christian?
3. When the text says that Adoniram was "going home to Plymouth to get some answers" (page 41), what kind of answers are being referred to?
4. How do you think Adoniram's spiritual journey might have been different if he had not been near Jacob Eames when Jacob died? Explain your answer.

Chapter Five

1. What is a heathen (page 52)? Use this word in a sentence.
2. How far did Adoniram and his friends walk from Andover to Bradford?

3. Why would Adoniram have found it surprising that Dr. Griffin supported his idea of becoming a missionary?
4. Do you think Adoniram was qualified to become America's first foreign missionary? Explain your answer.

Chapter Six

1. What does *pillaging* mean (page 63)? Use this word in a sentence.
2. What belongings did Adoniram retrieve from his cabin before the French privateers forced him onto their ship?
3. Why was it "a blow to almost everyone concerned" when the American Board had to ask the London Missionary Society for financial assistance (page 61)?
4. Why do you think Adoniram was the one chosen to go to England to ask for money to send out American missionaries?

Chapter Seven

1. What does *lucrative* mean (page 82)? Use this word in a sentence.
2. How much money did Mr. Norris leave the American Board?
3. Why did Adoniram and Ann think that the *Harmony* might be the last ship leaving American waters for some time?
4. Why do you think Adoniram felt such dread over saying good-bye to his friends and family?

Chapter Eight

1. What does *dejected* mean (page 89)? Use this word in a sentence.
2. What organization ruled over foreigners in India?
3. Why did William Carey caution Adoniram that it was "a noble goal of yours to go to Burma, though perhaps not one that is obtainable" (page 91)?
4. If you were Adoniram, would the information about Burma from William Carey cause your goals to change? Explain your answer.

Chapter Nine

1. What does *deplorable* mean (page 101)? Use this word in a sentence.
2. Where was the *Georgiana* bound?
3. Why did William Carey write to the American Baptists on behalf of the Judsons?
4. What do you think was the most discouraging thing that Adoniram faced in this chapter? Explain your answer.

Chapter Ten

1. What does *demeanor* mean (page 117)? Use this word in a sentence.
2. How long did it take the Judsons to receive their first letter from the United States?
3. Why was it so important for Adoniram and Ann to secure favor with the viceroy and the vicereine?
4. Do you think Adoniram would have been able to cope during the first year in Burma without Ann? Explain your answer.

Chapter Eleven

1. What is a tunic (page 124)? Use this word in a sentence.
2. In 1817, how many copies of Adoniram's tract were printed?
3. Why were Adoniram and Ann anxious at first when the vicereine came to visit after Roger's death?
4. Why do you think the Burmese people had so much trouble accepting that they could be both Burmese and Christian?

Chapter Twelve

1. What does *conspired* mean (page 134)? Use this word in a sentence.
2. Who convinced George Hough to move to Calcutta?
3. What did the officials mean when they threatened to write their report with George's own blood (page 140)?
4. Who do you think showed more courage while Adoniram was away: Ann Judson or George Hough? Explain your answer.

Chapter Thirteen

1. What does *prostrate* mean (page 157)? Use this word in a sentence.
2. How long did it take the missionaries to travel by boat from Rangoon to Ava?
3. Why were fewer Burmese people visiting the mission station under the new viceroy?
4. Adoniram knew it was a risk to visit King Bagyidaw in Ava. Do you think you would have taken this risk? Explain your answer.

Chapter Fourteen

1. What are reprisals (page 161)? Use this word in a sentence.
2. What type of surgery did Dr. Price specialize in?
3. Why was Adoniram convinced that Maung Shway-gnong would be put to death if he became a Christian?
4. By the end of the chapter, Adoniram had been in Burma for eight years. What is one important lesson you think he learned during this time, and how did he learn it?

Chapter Fifteen

1. What does *excruciating* mean (page 178)? Use this word in a sentence.
2. Adoniram was arrested because of his association with what other "foreigner"?
3. Why didn't Adoniram's old friends in Ava want to see him?
4. Which aspect of Adoniram's imprisonment do you think would be the most difficult to endure? Explain your answer.

Chapter Sixteen

1. What does *emaciated* mean (page 190)? Use this word in a sentence.
2. What did Ann do with the New Testament translation so that Adoniram could have it with him in prison?
3. Why did Adoniram sob when one of his former servants helped to support him while he was walking to Amarapura?

4. Do you think that Adoniram held out any hope that his New Testament translation might somehow be saved? Explain your answer.

Chapter Seventeen

1. What does *fortitude* mean (page 202)? Use this word in a sentence.
2. Who rescued Adoniram's pillow with the translated pages inside?
3. In 1831, there were 217 baptisms in Burma. To what did Adoniram attribute this new openness to Christianity?
4. In a short period of time, Adoniram faced the death of many people he loved. Why do you think he chose to continue his mission work in Burma?

Chapter Eighteen

1. What does *painstaking* mean (page 210)? Use this word in a sentence.
2. What nickname did the press give to Adoniram?
3. When Adoniram and Sarah were married, what made them unsure of how much time they would have together?
4. What do you think was the biggest challenge Adoniram faced upon his return to the United States? Explain your answer.

Chapter Nineteen

1. What does *impending* mean (page 224)? Use this word in a sentence.
2. What was the age difference between Adoniram and Emily?

3. Why was Adoniram confident that Emily was the answer to his prayers for someone to write Sarah's story?
4. Looking back on his life, what do you think Adoniram would rank as his proudest accomplishment? Why?

4

Student Explorations

Student explorations are a variety of activities that are appropriate for a wide range of learning styles. These activities consist of the following:

Essay Questions. These are questions that can be used as ideas for writing essays. Students can either be assigned a topic or choose their own from the list. The simplest essay topics appear first, followed in order by those that are more complex.

Creative Writing. This includes various types of writing such as newspaper articles, poems, letters, résumés, journals, and songs.

Hands-on Projects. These are various kinds of projects, such as charts and graphs, models, comic strips, family crests, mottoes, dioramas, book covers, and mobiles.

Audio/Visual Projects. These involve such activities as using a tape recorder to conduct a mock interview or to produce a radio play or commercial, or using still and video cameras to create dramatic presentations.

Arts and Crafts. These include a variety of art and craft forms used in Myanmar (Burma).

Language Examples. Some examples of words written in the Burmese language are given. Students can use them to make banners or place mats for the culminating event or in their hands-on projects. For example, they could use Burmese script in their design of a Judson family crest.

[Note on group projects: All the suggestions described below are individual learning activities. However, some of the activities have bracketed paragraphs such as this one that offer suggestions on how the activity can be adapted for class or group use.]

Essay Questions

1. Each of Adoniram Judson's three wives contributed to the work in Burma. Using examples from the book, explain each one's unique contribution.

2. Adoniram Judson encountered many obstacles when he went to Burma. Explain which two obstacles you think were the most difficult for him to deal with, and why.

3. There were many times when Adoniram Judson felt like giving up. Using examples from the book, explain how he was able to carry on.

4. Adoniram Judson was the United States' first Baptist missionary. Research your denomination's history of missions, and write an essay that explains how the organization was formed, its purpose, and the experiences of its early missionaries.

5. How and why did the British Empire impose itself on the land of Burma? How does that historical

background continue to influence Burmese society today?

6. Burma (now called Myanmar) is still a land where many people's human rights are violated. Using www.prayforburma.org (search for "The Forgotten People") and other websites, research this problem. Write an essay comparing and contrasting Adoniram Judson's experiences with what might happen to a Christian missionary working in Myanmar today.

Creative Writing

1. Imagine that Adoniram Judson kept a journal of his voyage to India and on to Burma. Write three to five entries in it, describing some of his experiences.

2. Choose a key event in Adoniram Judson's life, and write a newspaper article about it. For example, you might write about his imprisonment in Bayonne or his attempt to reach Chittagong. Be sure to include a catchy headline.
   [If you allocate different events to different students, your class can create an entire newspaper that covers the whole of Adoniram Judson's life.]

3. Imagine you are the Bible translation that Adoniram Judson was working on when war broke out. Write about your adventures and how you finally got back into his hands.

4. Adoniram Judson had no funeral service on the boat. Write a short speech that the captain could have read to the crew to tell them about the man they buried at sea.

5. Ann Judson supported her husband throughout many difficult situations. Choose one of these incidents, and write a poem about it from her point of view.

6. Study some photographs of the Burmese pagodas, and write a poem describing them.

Hands-on Projects

1. Make a poster map of Asia. Paste pictures on the map to represent what Adoniram Judson did in various places. For example, you might paste a picture of a printing press in Serampore, where he met William Carey, or a picture of a church at Moulmein to represent his church there.
   [This can be an individual or a group effort.]

2. Design a family crest for the Judson family. Write a brief explanation of why you chose each symbol.

3. Design a comic book based on several incidents from Adoniram Judson's life.

4. Using the websites listed in the Books and Resources section, design a travel brochure to encourage tourism in Myanmar today. Make sure it answers some of the basic questions a traveler might have. (You may want to look at travel brochures for other destinations to get ideas.)

5. Using papier-mâché or modeling clay, make a topographical model of Myanmar. Paint it and use toothpick flags to label major cities, rivers, mountains, neighboring countries, and seas. Put stars on the places where Adoniram Judson lived.

6. Draw a "Wanted" poster for Adoniram Judson that the French government could have circulated after he was smuggled out of the prison in Bayonne. (Make sure it shows what he looked like and what he was being held for.)

7. Select or make models of five objects that represent various stages in Adoniram Judson's life. Make a display explaining why you consider the objects to be significant. For example, you might draw a puzzle to represent his childhood love for enigmas or make an "old" pillow to represent the way the Bible translation was saved.
[Coordinate the "artifacts" and present them in a display. Have students prepare an audio tour of the artifacts telling how they reflect various aspects of Adoniram Judson's life.]

Audio/Visual Projects

1. Create a short television or radio spot inviting the public to your church to hear a presentation about Adoniram Judson.

2. Select several pages of the text that you think are very exciting. Read them onto a tape recorder and add appropriate sound effects for a dramatic presentation.

3. Create a television documentary called *Myanmar, the Unknown Land.* Start by interviewing a selection of people to find out what they know (or don't know) about Myanmar. Then use videotape, posters, photographs, and commentary to teach viewers about the country.

[This can be done as a group project by having various partners or teams assigned different areas, such as geography, history, religion, and neighboring countries.]

4. Create a "Jeopardy" game about Adoniram Judson's life and the places he visited. Stage it for your class and videotape it.

5. Create a series of five mock interviews with people who were significant in Adoniram Judson's life. Ask them questions about what they think of him and his missionary work. (For example, you might ask his university lecturer what kind of student he was, or his father-in-law, Mr. Hasseltine, why he allowed his daughter Ann to marry him.) Record these interviews on audiotape or videotape.

Arts and Crafts

1. Using a picture book on Myanmar as a guide, create two dolls (one boy and one girl) in national Burmese costume.

2. The Burmese people are famous for their gold overlay. Make a cross out of wood, bamboo, or clay, and try overlaying it with gold-colored foil.

3. The children of Myanmar make their own toys to play with, and one of their favorites is a kite. Make a kite, decorate it, and fly it. (Good patterns and ideas can be found in library books or at http://sewing.about.com/cs/kitemaking.)

4. The next section gives several examples of words written in the Burmese language. Use these words

to make banners, posters, and bookmarks, and use them on invitations or place mats for the culminating event.

Language Examples

Below are sentences written in Burmese.

Jesus loves you

သင့်ကို သခင်ယေရှု ချစ်သည်။

God is love

ဘုရားသခင်သည် ချစ်ခြင်းမေတ္တာ ဖြစ်သည်။

Hope in Christ

သခင်ယေရှု ထံမှာ မျှော်လင့်ခြင်းထားပါ။

You can also see samples of Burmese writing at www.chick.com (search for Burmese tract) and www.worldscriptures.org (click on "Language Listing," then "Burmese" to see the first page of the Gospel of John).

5

Community Links

Many communities have rich resources of people and places to which students can be exposed to help them learn about and appreciate other cultures. It is well worth the effort to find out what your community has to offer in regard to the unit you are studying. However, for centuries Myanmar has been one of the most closed countries in the world, so it is unlikely that you will find Burmese people, churches, or resources in your community. For your students to gain some idea of life there, you may want to look to Myanmar's neighbors for information. Myanmar is bordered by Bangladesh, India, China, Laos, and Thailand. Each of these cultures share many similarities with the Burmese, including geography, food, weather patterns, religions, and customs. For example, you may be able to visit an Asian church and interview some of its members, or you could tour a nearby Asian restaurant.

While it would be wonderful if you could take a field trip to visit some of these people and places, if you can't, it is often possible to have visitors come to the classroom. Whether you decide to take a field trip or invite a guest to your classroom, such activities need to be flanked by sound educational choices; otherwise, much of the educational value of the event will not be realized. The following three steps will help students derive the greatest educational value from a field trip or classroom visit.

Step One: Preparation.

Students should always research the topic before they begin a field trip or classroom interview. In doing so, they will be ready to ask intelligent questions based upon a sound knowledge of their topic. For example, if a class is going to visit a Thai restaurant, be sure the students know which dishes Thailand and Myanmar have in common. Knowing this, they can zero in on Burmese food at the restaurant.

As the teacher, you need to give the students a clear idea as to why they are going on the field trip and what they are expected to produce with their findings. For example, you might say to them, "We are going to visit a Thai restaurant. When we get back to class, you will be writing a poem about the food you ate."

Prior to the event, students should be encouraged to compile lists of questions to which they want answers, stemming from what they have already learned. They should carry a clipboard with them to write down answers, draw sketches, and note observations. (For less motivated students, a simple worksheet of activities to be completed on the field trip itself may be a good idea.) Such activities reinforce the idea that the field trip is a serious educational event and that the student is there to gather information, not just to be a sightseer.

Step Two: The Event

During the field trip or classroom visit, make sure that the students remain on task. Insist that they be respectful of property and other people at all times. Make sure that you have a spokesperson designated to thank whomever you talk to as well as the parents who help with the event.

Step Three: Processing and Reflection

Students should be given time to process the information they have gathered from their field trip or classroom visit and reflect on it, both individually and as a class. This can take many forms, including making flowcharts or diagrams of what they have learned, editing interviews for articles or audiovisual presentations, writing reports, and making booklets. Something as simple as a class book called *Did You Know?*, in which each student writes down one fact he or she learned from the field trip, can serve as an effective reflection tool.

Suggested Community Links

Asian Church. Locate an Asian church in your area. Call the pastor and ask permission to take your class for a visit. (Attending a Sunday service would be ideal if you can arrange it with the students' families.) Be sure to find out if the church has a dress code or any special customs that the students (and you) should be aware of. If attending a Sunday service is not possible, ask if you can visit the pastor on another day or if the pastor can come to school to speak to your class.

Chinatown. Perhaps you have a Chinatown in your area to visit. Here your students can get an idea of what living in Asia might be like. Have them pay attention to the smells, tastes, and sights around them. (Be sure to have specific learning expectations in place before you go so that the field trip does not become chaotic.)

Asian Restaurant. Arrange to visit an Asian restaurant during a nonbusy time of the day. (Thai or Laotian would be closest to the food eaten in Myanmar.) See if you can arrange ahead of time for the owner to talk to the class about preparing and eating Asian food. Eat lunch there, making sure the students try some foods that are new to them.

Burmese or East Asian People. People are some of the best resources of all. Are there any Burmese people in your town? (Probably the easiest way to find out is to contact either the Buddhist community or an East Asian Christian church.)

People Who Have Visited Myanmar. Although tourism is not a large industry in Myanmar, an increasing number of people have visited the country. If you find such a person, invite him or her to show slides or photos and other memorabilia from the trip.

Missionary Who Has Worked in Asia. If you can locate a missionary who has worked in Asia, invite him or her to your class to tell you about his or her experiences. Be sure to ask about the difficulty he or she had in adjusting to a different culture, and the various religious practices that were encountered. These can be compared and contrasted with Adoniram Judson's experiences.

Capital City: ______________________

Size of Country: ______________________

Population: ______________________

Main Religions:

	Name	Percentage of Population
1		
2		
3		
4		

Literacy Rate: ______________________

Main Exports: ______________________

BURMA FACT SHEET

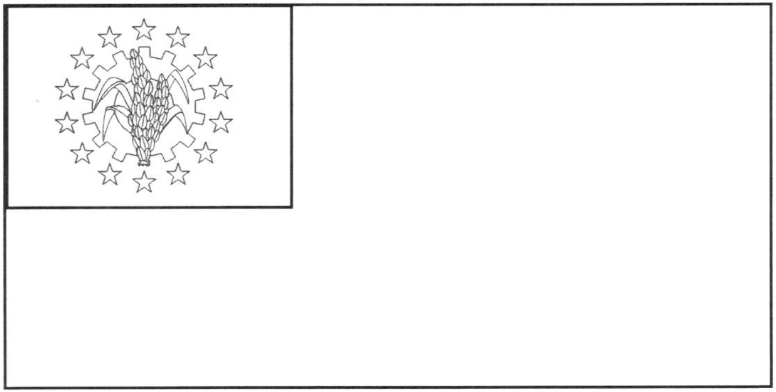

Southeast Asia

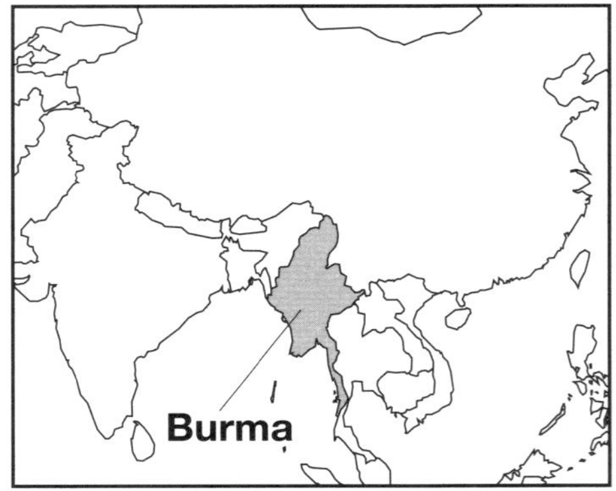

Official Name of Country: ______________________

Type of Government: ______________________

Current Head of State:

6

Social Studies

The social studies section is divided into four categories, each with suggestions on how to use the material given. The categories are briefly described below.

Places. This section covers significant places related to the story and named in the text of the book *Adoniram Judson: Bound for Burma.*

Terms/Vocabulary. This section gives ideas for studying some of the terms used in the book.

Geographical Characteristics. This section contains suggestions for mapping some of the physical characteristics of Burma.

Conceptual Questions. This section provides the teacher with conceptual social studies questions related to the book.

Places

These places are categorized by country. The page number where the place is first mentioned is in parentheses. Students can undertake a range of activities with these place names. They can

- Locate and mark the places on the relevant country map. (Maps for this purpose are located in the foldout section of this guide.)
- Note other points, such as their absolute location (latitude and longitude), then observe how this location compares to other locations mentioned in the book. For example, calculate which location is closer to the equator or the North Pole.
- Calculate the relative locations of various places mentioned in the book. For example, how far is it from Boston to Rangoon or from Calcutta to Ava?
- Explore how some of the place names have changed since the time Adoniram Judson lived, and give reasons for such changes.
- Pinpoint the places on a large wall map in the classroom. Students can then use index cards to write why various places are mentioned in the story. Each card could be pinned to the wall, with a length of yarn connecting it to the appropriate place on the map.

Places in the United States

Boston, Massachusetts (11)
Wenham, Massachusetts (14)
Salem, Massachusetts (21)
Saratoga Springs, New York (22)
Braintree, Massachusetts (22)
Plymouth, Massachusetts (23)
New Haven, Connecticut (23)
Providence, Rhode Island (24)
New York, New York (29)
Springfield, Massachusetts (32)
Sheffield, Massachusetts (32)
Albany, New York (32)
Andover, Massachusetts (42)
Bradford, Massachusetts (53)
Philadelphia, Pennsylvania (219)

Places in India

Calcutta (78)
Serampore (90)
Saugar (98)
Madras (102)
Andaman Islands (105)
Chittagong [now in Bangladesh] (132)
Masulipitam (135)

Places in Burma

Rangoon (90)
Ava (111)
Amarapura (154)
Yandabo (197)
Amherst (200)
Moulmein (206)

Other places

London, England (11)
Bayonne, France (67)
Le Passage, Spain (67)
Isle of France [now called Mauritius] (94)
Port Louis [now in Mauritius] (98)
Penang, Malaysia (102)
St. Helena Island (214)

Terms/Vocabulary

Following is a list of terms used in the book. The page number where the term is first used is in parentheses. The list covers terms ranging from the simple to the advanced. Students can use this list to

- Define and memorize the terms. You may find it helpful to asterisk or highlight in some way those terms you think are appropriate for your students. If they know the meaning of all but five of the terms, have them learn only those five. Conversely, if they are unfamiliar with most of the terms, choose a realistic number for each student to explore and learn.

- Produce an individual or class reference book of terms. Assign each student a number of terms to write a definition for or, where possible, draw a sketch of. From this research, a book of definitions can be made, with one page allotted for each definition. This book could be added to throughout the year. (Students may need a dictionary to help them with this activity.)
- Play reinforcement games such as Go Fish. To do this, draw some of the sketched definitions from the list compiled in the point above onto index cards, and have students take turns pairing them with written definitions.

Terms/vocabulary

foreign (12)
privateers (13)
starboard (14)
longboats (64)
horizon (67)
Union Jack (67)
bayonet (68)
sloop (73)
delta (87)
enclave (91)
uncharted (93)
slavery (101)
plantation (101)
straits (102)
pagoda (106)
pilgrims (107)
peasants (107)
primitive (107)
superstitious (107)
smallpox (111)
vaccination (112)
viceroy (115)
diplomat (117)
Buddhist (126)
reincarnation (126)
dysentery (135)
treaty (197)
imported (201)
exported (201)
sandbar (212)
barque (228)

Geographical Characteristics

Have students use an atlas to locate the following and mark them on the blank map of Myanmar (Burma) from the foldout section in the center of the book:

- The following three major rivers in Myanmar, their sources, and their courses: Irrawaddy, Salween, and Sittang
- The following three mountain ranges: Chin Hills, Kumon Range, and Shan Plateau
- The five major geographical regions: Northern Region, Western Region, Central Region, Shan Plateau, and Tanintharyi coastal strip
- The following five cities: Rangoon, Mandalay, Moulmein, Pegu, and Bassein
- The latitude and longitude lines that bisect Myanmar
- The seas and oceans that border Myanmar: Indian Ocean, Bay of Bengal, Andaman Sea, and Gulf of Martaban
- The countries with which Myanmar shares borders: Bangladesh, India, China, Laos, and Thailand
- Hkakabo Razi, the highest point in Myanmar at 19,296 feet (5,881 meters)

Conceptual Questions

The following questions are ordered from the simple to the complex. Using these questions, you could ask students to

- Write one or more paragraphs to answer each question.
- Present an oral report to the class on one of the questions.
- Discuss the answer(s) to a question or questions in a group context.

Questions to ponder

1. Locate and name two countries that are larger than Myanmar, two that are about the same size, and two that are smaller.
2. How large is Myanmar compared to the United States?
3. What is the population of Myanmar compared to the population of the United States?
4. Myanmar has been in a state of political turmoil for many years. Using encyclopedias, history books, and contemporary news articles and reports, explore the roots of the country's political problems.
5. Draw a map of Myanmar's main rivers and investigate their role in the country's economy.
6. Locate the countries that border Myanmar. Research the relationships between these neighboring countries and Myanmar, and explain the reasons for such relationships.

7

Related Themes to Explore

Any unit study has natural links to many other topics that can also be explored. While it is impossible to pursue all such links in this context, the spoke diagram on the next page shows some related topics that students might find interesting to study in conjunction with Adoniram Judson.

There are two ways you might like to integrate some of these links into your classroom. Some teachers and parents have the flexibility to choose the topics their students study and even alter their selections partway through the year. If you are able to do this, use the theme wheel to help identify other topics you might like to explore following this unit. For example, after studying Adoniram Judson, your class might become interested in Buddhism or the history of missions in America.

Other teachers and parents are locked into a less flexible curriculum. If this is your situation, you may still have the ability to change the order in which various topics are taught. Look through the topics listed to see whether any coincide with topics you have already scheduled for later in the year. Consider the possibility of scheduling the teaching of these topics closer to this unit so that cross-curriculum learning can take place.

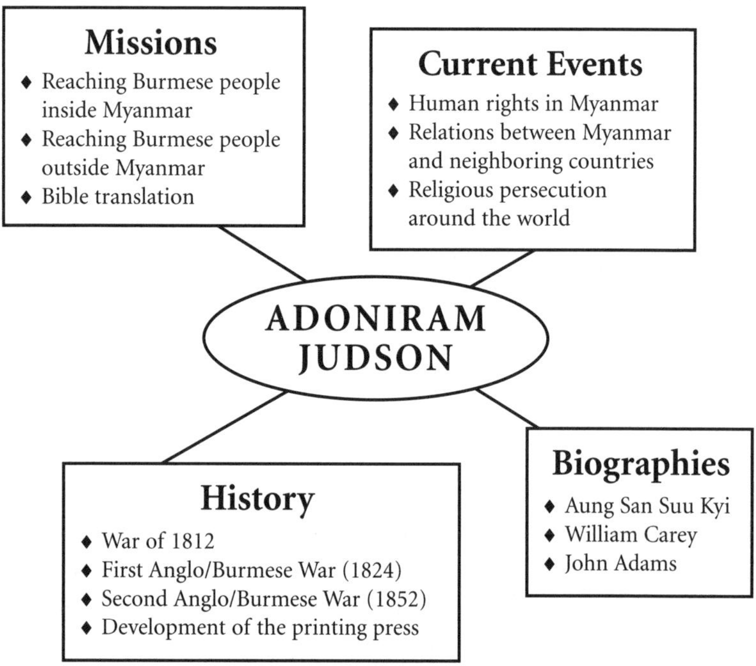

8

Culminating Event

As adults, we like to have a reason to learn something. We learn a new computer program so that we can balance our checking account, a song so that we can sing it at a wedding, or the rudiments of another language so that we are able to find our way around in a foreign country. Students have the same need for purpose in their learning. It is valid but not very motivating to tell a student that he or she needs to gather and learn information to pass a test or move up a grade. It is much more motivating for a student when he or she has some other, more meaningful, goal in mind. This goal can be a specific forum through which each student can express his or her newly acquired knowledge. We believe that part of a teacher's role is to provide such a forum, which we call the culminating event.

As the name implies, the culminating event marks the end of the unit study and gives a sense of closure to the topic. It also serves to put the students' new knowledge into a larger context that can be shared with others.

The culminating event can be as simple as inviting the class next door (or the homeschooled children down the street) to come and hear poems and stories and view your students' written work. Conversely, the event could be as involved as hosting a parent/neighborhood dinner featuring Burmese songs and games, and plays and presentations on the life and achievements of Adoniram Judson and the places where he served.

No matter how simple or elaborate the culminating event is, make sure you have the broad outline in mind before planning the other activities for your unit study, as the two are integrally linked.

Idea Sparks

Food. Prepare and serve regional food. Fruits and vegetables grown and eaten in Myanmar include eggplant, okra, chayote, strawberries, avocados, oranges, mangoes, pears, pineapples, watermelons, and jackfruit. Meats include all kinds of fish, shrimp, and other shellfish, and smaller amounts of pork or chicken (beef is scarce). Food is often curried or very spicy, and rice is served with every meal. For recipes see the following websites:

www.myanmars.net/people/recipe.htm
http://Asiarecipe.com/burma.html

Beverages. Drink buffalo milk, fruit juice, tea, or coffee. (These are served with canned sweetened condensed milk.)

Table Manners. The oldest person present or head of the family always eats first. Food is eaten with the right hand. All the courses are put on the table at once, and people choose whatever they feel like eating. The table is normally low to the ground, and people sit either directly on the ground or on low stools. Talking with your mouth full of food, eating slowly, slouching, and sighing are all considered bad manners at the table.

Music. Play traditional Burmese music in the background to set the mood. Many libraries stock ethnic music selections, or you can download music from the following website:

http://search.asiaco.com/Myanmar/Personal_Home_Pages/

Oral Presentations. Students can present poems, essays, reports, speeches, reviews, journals, and devotions that they have written during the course of the unit study.

Displays. Display other work, including artwork, map work, models, newspapers, and video interviews.

Clothing. Students can dress in Burmese clothing for the event. Both males and females traditionally wear the *longyi,* which is a long, straight skirt. Boys' skirts are normally checked or plain and tied in front, while girls' skirts are flowered or patterned and tied at the side. Boys wear a shirt and jacket on top, and girls wear a plain blouse. Both wear flip-flops or open sandals. They put a yellow paste called *tanaka* on their cheeks, which they use as a sunscreen. Although the paste is made from the branches of a special tree, you could simulate the look with flour, water, and yellow food coloring.

Appendix A

Books and Resources

This appendix is divided into six sections: (1) other biographies of Adoniram Judson, (2) related books, (3) related books in the Christian Heroes: Then & Now series and the Heroes of History series, (4) a related documentary, (5) related articles from *National Geographic,* and (6) related Internet sites.

Some of the books about Adoniram Judson are written at a higher reading level than books in the Christian Heroes: Then & Now series and therefore would be useful for a teacher to read for his or her own information as background for the unit. Students learn best by example, so consider reading one adult book to enrich your own understanding of the topic. Resources for younger children are also included, making it easy for younger family members or less capable readers to participate in the unit study at their own reading level.

Some of the books listed here are more difficult to obtain than others. If they are not available at your local Christian bookstore, many of the titles can be located in secondhand bookstores or on the Internet. Most of the titles are also available through the national interlibrary loan service.

Other Biographies of Adoniram Judson

The biographies listed on the bibliography page of *Adoniram Judson: Bound for Burma* are listed here. Each listing has basic information on how to locate the book, including its ISBN. The approximate intended age level of the reader is also given, along with the number of pages in each book and some comments to help you decide whether or not to include the book in your unit study.

TITLE: *To the Golden Shore*
Author: Courtney Anderson
Publisher: Little, Brown and Co., 1988
ISBN: 0817011218
Age Level: Adult, 530 pages

Synopsis: This is a thorough biography of Judson. It covers all aspects of his life, including his family history.

Comments: This is the definitive modern biography of Judson. It is filled with interesting information and is easy to follow.

TITLE: *Adoniram Judson: Following God's Plan*
Author: Fern Neal Stocker
Publisher: Moody Press, 1986
ISBN: 0802443842
Age Level: 8–10 years, 122 pages

Synopsis: This biography is a "guessing book" that offers the reader several scenarios of what decision Judson will make in specific situations.

Comments: The guessing parts might be somewhat distracting (up to three per page), but otherwise the story reads well.

Related Books

Listed in this section are other books that fit around the life of Adoniram Judson. The listings include the ISBN, age level, and relevant comments.

Of course, there are many other books that relate in some way to this topic. Inside the back cover of this unit study guide you may want to record the titles of other books you find particularly helpful.

TITLE: *Ann of Ava*
Author: Ethel Daniels Hubbard
Publisher: Ayer Co., 1941
ISBN: 0836980840
Age Level: 10 years and up, 185 pages

Synopsis: This is a biography of Judson's first wife, Ann. Many historians believe she was essential to his eventual success.

Comments: Young readers may find the wording a bit flowery and moralizing, but the story is relevant and interesting nonetheless.

TITLE: *Imprisoned in the Golden City* (Trailblazer Series)
Authors: Dave, Neta, and Julian Jackson
Publisher: Bethany House, 1993
ISBN: 1556612699
Age Level: 8–12 years, 160 pages

Synopsis: This is the story of two Burmese girls who were taken in by the Judsons around the time that Adoniram was imprisoned.

Comments: Although the story is fictionalized, the Judsons did take in two Burmese foster daughters, and the events that happened to Adoniram are portrayed accurately. This book will help younger readers understand Burma and the challenges that the Judsons faced.

TITLE: *Aung San Suu Kyi: Standing Up for Democracy in Burma*
Authors: Bettina Ling and Charlotte Bunch
Publisher: The Feminist Press at the City University of New York, 1999
ISBN: 1558611967
Age Level: 10 years and up, 112 pages

Synopsis: This is a biography of Aung San Suu Kyi, Nobel Peace Prize winner in 1991. Born in 1945, Suu was only two when her father, General Aung San, the emerging leader of a democratic Burma, was gunned down. Suu followed her father into politics and today is the leading voice for democracy in Myanmar.

Comments: This book gives an excellent look at the political and social conditions in Myanmar today, as well as their historical context.

Related Christian Heroes: Then & Now and Heroes of History Books

TITLE: *William Carey: Obliged to Go*
Authors: Janet and Geoff Benge
Publisher: YWAM Publishing, 1998
ISBN: 1576581470
Age Level: 10 years and up

Comments: William Carey (1761–1834) was one of the first missionaries to India. He persevered through personal trials, including the death of two wives and the ravages of fire and floods. Although he had little formal schooling, he took on the task of translating the Bible into Bengali and was eventually recognized as a leading Bengali and Sanskrit scholar. Carey helped Judson when he arrived in India on his way to Burma, and his mission at Serampore supported Judson through his first years in Rangoon.

TITLE: *John Adams: Independence Forever*
Authors: Janet and Geoff Benge
Publisher: Emerald Books, 2002
ISBN: 1883002516
Age Level: 10 years and up, 215

Comments: John Adams was a Yankee who featured largely in the American Revolution and the founding of the United States. He served overseas as an ambassador to the French and became the second U.S. president. Judson lived for a while in Braintree, where John Adams also lived. Each time they passed the Adamses' home, Judson's father would encourage his son that he too could rise to greatness.

Related Documentary

Listed in this section is a documentary relevant to Adoniram Judson. This film is not MPA rated, and as with all unfamiliar material, it is prudent to preview it before showing it to the class.

Movies and documentaries are particularly useful in showing the visual details of another place and time period. As students watch, encourage them to study the clothing, weather, crops, terrain, and other geographical factors shown in the documentary.

TITLE: *Raising the Bamboo Curtain: Emerging Burma and Cambodia*
Publisher: Questar Video

Type: Documentary
Length: 60 minutes
Year: 1995

Comments: Narrated by Martin Sheen, the first half of this video focuses on Burma. It tells a lot about the current political situation there, as well as British colonialism. The video has great shots of the Irrawaddy River and the pagodas Judson would have seen often. The second half on Cambodia shows some disturbing scenes of the Khmer Rouge's rule, including images of many skulls.

Related *National Geographic* Articles

Many magazines have articles related to this topic. We have chosen to reference *National Geographic* because it can provide contemporaneous commentary on many events and because it is widely available in libraries and schools throughout the country. (*National Geographics* from 1888–2000 are available in their entirety in a CD-ROM set.)

These articles and their accompanying photographs represent just some of those available that bear on aspects of Adoniram Judson's life. They can be used in a variety of ways to support and reinforce this unit study. For example, you could have students read the July 1995 article "Burma: The Richest of Poor Countries" and have them compare and contrast the photographs and descriptions in the text with the October 1909 article "Notes on Burma." They could produce a Venn diagram that highlights the similarities and differences that have occurred over eighty-five years in Burma.

TITLE: "Burma: The Richest of Poor Countries"
Issue Date: July 1995, pages 70–97

Description: This is an excellent article by a Western journalist who spent his childhood in Burma and returned to record his impressions of how it had changed. It contains a lot of information on the Burmese government and a resource map.

TITLE: "Time and Again in Burma"
Issue Date: July 1984, pages 90–121

Description: This article is a great general introduction to Burma and its culture. It contains lots of interesting photographs, though one of self-flagellation may disturb some students.

TITLE: "Burma's Leg Rowers and Floating Farms"
Issue Date: June 1974, pages 826–845

Description: This article offers a fascinating look at the lives of people who live along the shores of Inle Lake. Their culture has not changed significantly for hundreds of years.

TITLE: "Pagan: On the Road to Mandalay"
Issue Date: March 1971, pages 343–365

Description: This article was written by one of the first journalists allowed into Pagan since socialist rule. The descriptions and photographs show a land that is unchanged since Judson's time.

TITLE: "Burma, Gentle Neighbor of India and Red China"
Issue Date: February 1963, pages 153–199

Description: This is another excellent article on Burma, written a year after General Ne Win led a coup d'état and began the process of making Burma a socialist state. The article covers many of the diverse cultures within the country.

TITLE: "The 5,000 Temples of Pagan: Burma's Sacred City Is a Place of Enchantment in the Midst of Ruins"
Issue Date: October 1931, pages 444–462

Description: This article examines the amazing temples of Pagan and gives a detailed look at the capricious men who have ruled Burma through the centuries.

TITLE: "Untoured Burma"
Issue Date: July 1913, pages 835–853

Description: This article describes a trip into Burma. It reflects the colonial viewpoint of the time, offering interesting insights into the way the rest of the world viewed Burma.

TITLE: "Notes on Burma"
Issue Date: October 1909, pages 841–866

Description: This is a general article on Burma. It was written sixty years after Judson's death, but little had changed during that time. It contains good black-and-white photographs of scenes Judson would have encountered frequently.

Related Internet Sites

The following websites may have been updated since this guide was published, and as a result, they may contain information not reviewed here. Because of this, it is vital that you investigate them before allowing your students to view them.

www.wholesomewords.org/missions/biojudson.html

This is the online biography of Judson by his son Edward (who was born to his second wife, Sarah). It was first published in 1894 and has some excellent quotes from Judson's journals and those of his wives. It also tracks the early development of the two mission societies he was involved with.

www.lonelyplanet.com/destinations/south_east_asia/myanmar

This site explains Myanmar for the prospective traveler. It tracks things like weather, currency, visa requirements, tourist attractions, and festivals.

http://private.addcom.de/asiaphoto/burma/burmapage.htm

This site contains good general information on the culture and history of Burma and the current social situation, including birth and death rates, population, and government.

www.myanmar.com

This is the official website of the Myanmar government. It has links to all government departments, the national newspaper online, and a variety of historic, religious, and current information. Understandably, it is heavily weighted to portray the Burmese people as content with their government.

www.state.gov/www/global/human_rights/1998_hrp_report/burma.html

This is the State Department's assessment of human rights in Burma. The language is specific, and some of the examples are disturbing, but it would be useful for older students to review (especially in contrast to the Myanmar government's official site).

www.hoteltravel.com/myanmar/

This website gives information for the traveler, including currency exchange, weather, maps, city guides, and accommodations.

www.prayforburma.org

This website offers a Christian perspective of the problems in Myanmar and gives prayer requests. Search for "The Forgotten People" for an interesting look at the Karen people today. This site contains good photographs.

http://internationalbibles.com/catalog/bibles/publishers/abs/103789.htm

This is the International Bibles website, where you can purchase a copy of Judson's translation of the Bible into Burmese.

www.chick.com

This is the Chick Christian Tract website. It has one tract, "The Tycoon," available for reading in Burmese.

www.worldscriptures.org

Click on "Language Listing" then "Burmese" at this site to see the first page of the Gospel of John in the Burmese script.

http://search.asiaco.com/Myanmar/Personal_Home_Pages/

This is an umbrella site for many changing homepages of people and organizations that have to do with Myanmar. In it you can find individuals describing their life in Myanmar, poems, music, short stories, and many other interesting items.

Appendix B

Answers to Chapter Questions

Chapter One

1. Gunwales are the upper edges of a ship's sides.
2. The other two passengers on the *Packet* spoke Spanish.
3. It was especially dangerous to be aboard a British ship because there was a war going on between Britain and France, and French ships had a reputation for plundering British ships.

Chapter Two

1. An enigma is a mystery or puzzle.
2. Adoniram's father was a preacher.
3. Adoniram froze in terror because he knew his father would be angry with him for going behind his back to mail the letter.

Chapter Three

1. *Iniquity* means sin or wickedness.
2. Adoniram took the *Clermont,* a steamboat, from Albany to New York City.
3. Admitting to his father that he was a Deist would have put an end to Adoniram's college career because his father would have refused to allow him to stay at that university.

Chapter Four

1. A chaplain is a member of the clergy who works for an institution such as an army or a corporation.
2. Adoniram became a Christian on December 2, 1808.
3. The text is referring to answers to spiritual questions.

Chapter Five

1. A heathen is a person who does not acknowledge the God of the Bible.
2. Adoniram and his friends walked ten miles from Andover to Bradford.
3. Adoniram would have found Dr. Griffin's support surprising because he had turned down Dr. Griffin's offer to become his assistant pastor.

Chapter Six

1. *Pillaging* means raiding or looting.
2. Adoniram retrieved his three Bibles and his letter from Ann.
3. This was a blow to the American Board because tension still existed between Britain and the United States following the American Revolutionary War.

Chapter Seven

1. *Lucrative* means profitable or richly rewarding.
2. Mr. Norris left the American Board thirty thousand dollars.
3. They thought that this might be the last ship to leave for some time because America and Britain were gearing up for war with each other.

Chapter Eight

1. *Dejected* means sad or cast down in spirits.
2. The East India Company ruled over foreigners in India.
3. William Carey gave this caution because he knew about the Burmese king's dislike for foreigners and the harsh punishments for missionaries.

Chapter Nine

1. *Deplorable* means dreadful or terrible.
2. The *Georgiana* was bound for Rangoon, Burma.
3. William Carey wrote to the American Baptists because he was a well-known Baptist missionary.

Chapter Ten

1. *Demeanor* means manner or attitude.
2. It took the Judsons three years and seven months to receive their first letter from the United States.
3. It was important for them to secure favor with the viceroy and the vicereine because they had absolute authority and the Judsons' missionary efforts would be influenced by them.

Chapter Eleven

1. A tunic is a long, simple garment.
2. In 1817, one thousand copies of the tract were printed.
3. They were anxious at first because they thought they might have offended her and they knew that there were harsh punishments for offending authority figures in Burma.

Chapter Twelve

1. *Conspired* means plotted or schemed.
2. George's wife, Phebe, convinced him to move to Calcutta.
3. They meant they would kill him if he did not cooperate with them.

Chapter Thirteen

1. *Prostrate* means lying facedown in submission.
2. It took them a month to travel from Rangoon to Ava.
3. Fewer Burmese people were visiting the missionaries because the new viceroy was much less open to foreigners and their religion than the previous viceroy had been.

Chapter Fourteen

1. Reprisals are acts of revenge or retaliation.
2. Dr. Price specialized in cataract operations.
3. Adoniram was convinced that Maung Shway-gnong would be put to death because he was a Buddhist scholar and the Burmese leaders would fear that other Burmese people would follow his example.

Chapter Fifteen

1. *Excruciating* means agonizing or unbearable.
2. Adoniram was arrested because of his association with Henry Gouger.
3. They did not want to see him because they suspected him of being a spy.

Chapter Sixteen

1. *Emaciated* means thin or weakened.
2. Ann sewed the translation into a pillow so that Adoniram could have it with him in prison.
3. Adoniram sobbed because, after enduring torture in prison, he was overwhelmed by his former servant's act of kindness.

Chapter Seventeen

1. *Fortitude* means strength or courage.
2. Maung Ing rescued the pillow with the translated pages inside.
3. Adoniram attributed this new openness to Christianity to the war between Great Britain and Burma.

Chapter Eighteen

1. *Painstaking* means meticulous or careful.
2. The press gave Adoniram the nickname the "Saint of Burma."
3. The fact that so many missionaries they knew had died made them unsure how long each of them would live.

Chapter Nineteen

1. *Impending* means approaching in the near future.

2. The age difference between Adoniram and Emily was twenty-seven years.
3. Adoniram was confident that Emily was the answer to his prayers because she was an author, a Baptist, and one who was familiar with Sarah's story.

Also from Janet and Geoff Benge...

More adventure-filled biographies for ages 10 to 100!

Christian Heroes: Then & Now

Gladys Aylward: The Adventure of a Lifetime • 1-57658-019-9
Nate Saint: On a Wing and a Prayer • 1-57658-017-2
Hudson Taylor: Deep in the Heart of China • 1-57658-016-4
Amy Carmichael: Rescuer of Precious Gems • 1-57658-018-0
Eric Liddell: Something Greater Than Gold • 1-57658-137-3
Corrie ten Boom: Keeper of the Angels' Den • 1-57658-136-5
William Carey: Obliged to Go • 1-57658-147-0
George Müller: The Guardian of Bristol's Orphans • 1-57658-145-4
Jim Elliot: One Great Purpose • 1-57658-146-2
Mary Slessor: Forward into Calabar • 1-57658-148-9
David Livingstone: Africa's Trailblazer • 1-57658-153-5
Betty Greene: Wings to Serve • 1-57658-152-7
Adoniram Judson: Bound for Burma • 1-57658-161-6
Cameron Townsend: Good News in Every Language • 1-57658-164-0
Jonathan Goforth: An Open Door in China • 1-57658-174-8
Lottie Moon: Giving Her All for China • 1-57658-188-8
John Williams: Messenger of Peace • 1-57658-256-6
William Booth: Soup, Soap, and Salvation • 1-57658-258-2
Rowland Bingham: Into Africa's Interior • 1-57658-282-5
Ida Scudder: Healing Bodies, Touching Hearts • 1-57658-285-X
Wilfred Grenfell: Fisher of Men • 1-57658-292-2
Loren Cunningham: Into All the World • 1-57658-199-3
Lillian Trasher: The Greatest Wonder in Egypt • 1-57658-305-8

Heroes of History

George Washington Carver: From Slave to Scientist • 1-883002-78-8
Abraham Lincoln: A New Birth of Freedom • 1-883002-79-6
Meriwether Lewis: Off the Edge of the Map • 1-883002-80-X
George Washington: True Patriot • 1-883002-81-8
William Penn: Liberty and Justice for All • 1-883002-82-6
Harriet Tubman: Freedombound • 1-883002-90-7
John Adams: Independence Forever • 1-883002-51-6
Clara Barton: Courage under Fire • 1-883002-50-8
Daniel Boone: Frontiersman • 1-932096-09-4
Theodore Roosevelt: An American Original • 1-932096-10-8

Unit Study Curriculum Guides are available for select biographies.

Heroes for Young Readers...

Introduce children to the exciting true stories of Christian heroes with rhyming text and vivid color illustrations! For ages 6 and up.

Author: Renee Taft Meloche • Illustrator: Bryan Pollard

Children, parents, and teachers love the adventurous Christian Heroes: Then and Now biographies and unit study curriculum guides. Now Heroes for Young Readers introduces younger children to the lives of Christian heroes! Whether reading for themselves or being read to, children love the captivating rhyming poems and unforgettable color illustrations of the Heroes for Young Readers series.

Gladys Aylward: Daring to Trust • 1-57658-228-0
Nate Saint: Heavenbound • 1-57658-229-9
Eric Liddell: Running for a Higher Prize • 1-57658-230-2
George Müller: Faith to Feed Ten Thousand • 1-57658-232-9
Amy Carmichael: Rescuing the Children • 1-57658-233-7
Mary Slessor: Courage in Africa • 1-57658-237-X
Corrie ten Boom: Shining in the Darkness • 1-57658-231-0
William Carey: Bearer of Good News • 1-57658-236-1
Hudson Taylor: Friend of China • 1-57658-234-5
David Livingstone: Courageous Explorer • 1-57658-238-8
Adoniram Judson: A Grand Purpose • 1-57658-240-X
Betty Greene: Flying High • 1-57658-239-6

...and more coming soon!

Picture books all ages will treasure.
Hardcover editions!